Phoenix
and the valley of the sun

a p h o t o g r a p h i c p o r t r a i t

First published in the United States of America by
Twin Lights Publishers, Inc.
10 Hale Street
Rockport, Massachusetts 01966
Telephone: (978) 546-7398
http://www.twinlightspub.com

ISBN 1-885435-28-2

10 9 8 7 6 5 4 3 2 1

Book design by
SYP Design & Production, Inc.
http://www.sypdesign.com

Cover Photo by: Paul Scharbach
Back Cover Photos by: Gary J. Cooper,
Barbara A. Mangels, and Eddie Ellis

Printed in China

Other titles in the Photographic Portrait series:

Cape Ann
Kittery to the Kennebunks
The Mystic Coast, Stonington to New London
The White Mountains
Boston's South Shore
Upper Cape Cod
The Rhode Island Coast
Greater Newburyport
Portsmouth and Coastal New Hampshire
Naples, Florida
Sarasota, Florida
The British Virgin Islands
Portland, Maine
Mid and Lower Cape Cod
The Berkshires
Boston
Camden, Maine
Sanibel and Captiva Islands
San Diego's North County Coast
Newport Beach, California

Sales Representative:
Warren Salinger
Telephone: (480) 288-0738

C O N T E N T S

An extremely successful country music ballad that once surged to the top of the music charts proclaimed in its title that, "There Is No Arizona." But of course there is, big-time! And at the Grand Canyon State's vibrant core, Phoenix, its capital city, rises proudly in the center of The Valley of the Sun.

With a population of 1,321,000 people according to the most recent census figures, Phoenix has become the nation's sixth largest city, a far cry from its origin as a hay camp in 1866. Sky Harbor, its constantly growing airport and point of entry into the Phoenix area for many of its visitors and immigrants, logged 35.8 million passengers in 2000. This was an increase of seven percent over the previous year, making it the ninth busiest airport in the United States and the fifteenth most active in the world. When ranked by its 638,848 take-offs and landings, its worldwide place is fourth.

Phoenix and The Valley of the Sun are one with a total metropolitan area population of just under three million people, accounting for sixty percent of those living in the state. The Valley runs roughly one hundred miles from east to west and often stretches ninety-five miles south to north, containing an area of some 9,000 square miles. Its boundaries are generally the mountains that define it—the Maricopa and Sand Tank Mountains to the southwest, McDowell Mountain and the Mazatzal Mountains to the north and northeast, the Goldfields and the famed Superstitions to the east. Picacho Peak, just past Casa Grande to the southeast of Phoenix, provides closure in that direction. Four Peaks, often snow covered during the winter months and measuring 7,645 feet in altitude, provides sharp contrast to The Valley's desert floor.

The entire area is situated in the Sonoran Desert, seemingly ruled by the stately saguaro cactus, which also provides Arizona with its state flower. But, contrary to the images that the word "desert" might conjure up, The Valley of the Sun is an area filled with unusual plant and animal life, much of which is reflected in the beautiful photographs that follow.

Skies are clear or only partly cloudy 81 percent of the time and rainfall averages just seven inches per year, occurring mostly during the August monsoons. But winter can bring additional moisture as well and the more it rains then, the stronger the display of wildflowers in the spring. Though triple digit temperatures are not uncommon in the summer, every Arizonian will give you their well-rehearsed reply: "But it's a dry heat!"

It is impossible to visit or live in the Phoenix area without feeling the influence of the Native American culture and heritage. This is one of the major benefits of life here. And just as the mountains are visible from just about everywhere in Arizona, so is the history and the centuries old wisdom of its Native American citizens.

Whether you are here for the first time, have come often before, or are a permanent resident, you will like the photographs in this book, a small number judged the best of the hundreds submitted.

This is big sky country, combining the best of our Native American and Old West experiences and history with the state of the art of a modern American metropolitan area. Phoenix and The Valley of the Sun offer a distinctly western life style nurtured by an infrastructure and a cultural base necessary for a world class environment.

This is, *Phoenix and The Valley of the Sun: A Photographic Portrait.*

Acknowledgement

Twin Lights Publishers wishes to thank all of the photographers who submitted their work for our consideration. Because of space limitations, we were unable to include many excellent photographs in *Phoenix and the Valley of the Sun: A Photographic Portrait.* Phoenix is a fertile area for many talented resident professional and amateur photographers. The natural beauty attracts visitors to record its special qualities at all times of the year.

Special thanks go to Warren and Martha Salinger who organized and supervised the photography contest. Their efficiency and thoroughness made the judging of over 800 entries a less difficult task.

Thanks go to the judges of the Phoenix Regional Photography Contest, Margaret Dixon, Thorne E. Schubert, Ph.D., and Ronda A. Moffit, PH.D. We are pleased with their selections and are indebted to them.

We are grateful to Warren Salinger, author of several books and a consultant in corporate fund raising, who has written the introduction and the captions for the photographs. In writing the captions, he has found evocative titles and added facts to bring out the history and local color
for each photograph. We think he has given an added dimension to the book.

Finally, our thanks go to designer Sara Day who has created a beautiful book.

First Prize

Old Reflections
PAUL SCHARBACH
RB-67, FUJICHROME, F-11 @ 1/60TH

To know where you're going, you must remember where you've been. One of Phoenix' oldest landmarks, the Security Building, is reflected in the city skyline's Valley National Bank Building, its tallest structure. This juxtaposition also reflects the city's commitment to its historic past.

Paul Scharbach is a rarity in The Valley of the Sun—a native! Born and raised in Phoenix, he has been a professional photographer for more than twenty years, freelancing for part of that time while also working with Honeywell Aerospace. His main focus today is aircraft stock photography and computerized digital photo work. Downtown Phoenix has always been a photographic focal point for him.

The father of two, Paul is an avid hiker and biker (the pedal kind) for whom Phoenix and The Valley, with their endless offerings of mountains and trails, provide the perfect outdoor settings in which to enjoy the family's preferred lifestyle. We salute his professional skills!

Second Prize

Phoenix Sunset
PAUL SCHARBACH
4 X 5 VIEW CAMERA, F-16 @ 10 SECONDS

Downtown Phoenix, located at the core
of The Valley of the Sun, glistens in a
beautifully receding Arizona sunset.
Though the building's lights have just
come on, they are no match for
nature's art.

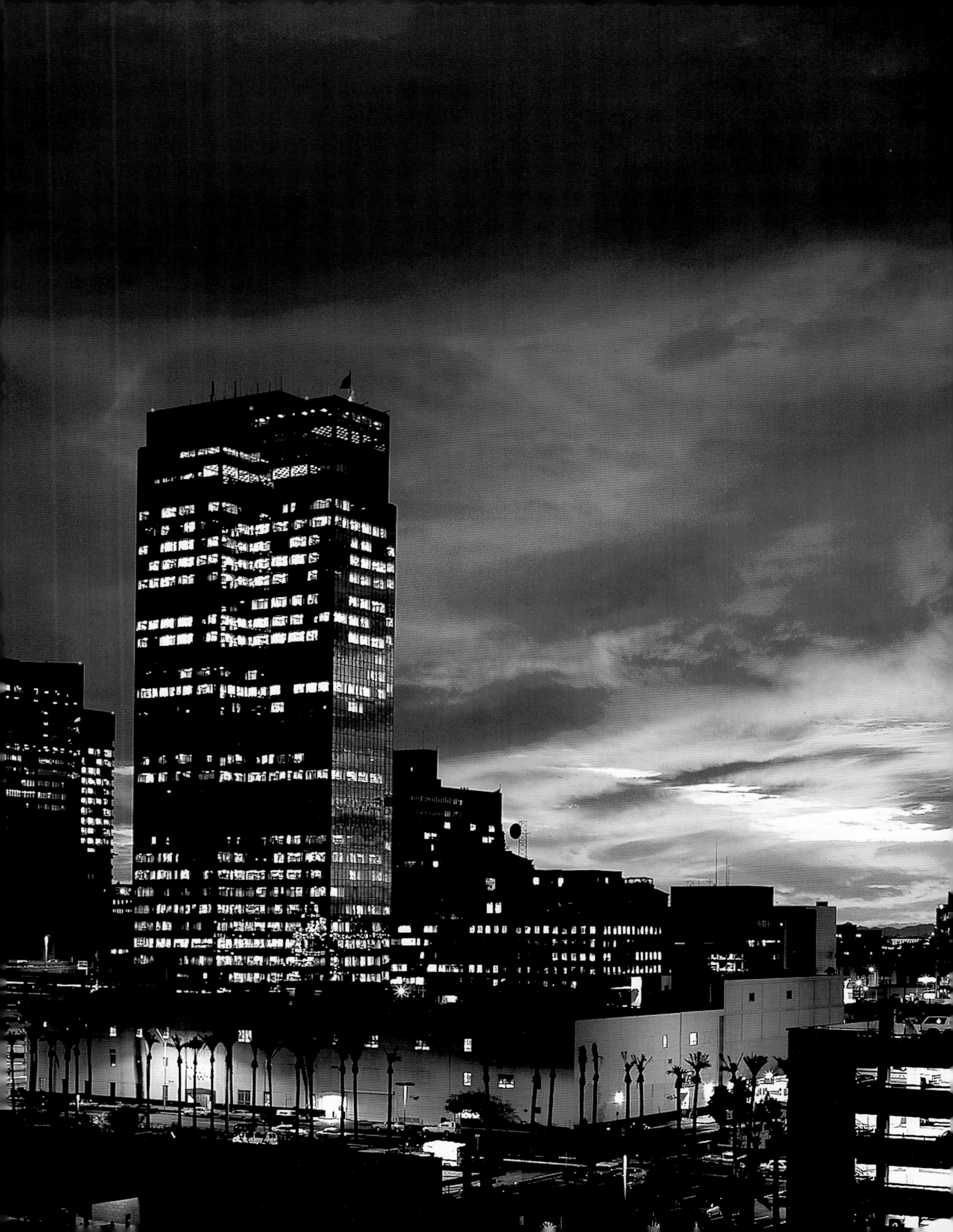

Gold Canyon Sunset

ANGELO (ANDY) VALENTI
NIKON F, KODAK GOLD 200, F-22 @ 1/250TH

Gold Canyon is situated some forty miles east of the center of Phoenix, astride Route 60 which leads to the copper mining cities of Superior and Globe. Nestled at the base of the Superstition Mountains, it is laced with hiking trails that often provide stunning sunset views like this one.

A seven year resident of Mountainbrook Village, an "active adult retirement community," **Andy Valenti** came to The Valley of the Sun from Thousand Oaks, California. His career commitment was in the field of medical technology but photography has captured his creative initiatives since he was a kid and he did a good deal of freelance photography while living and working in California. In addition to his camera work, his hobbies include ham radio, arts and sciences and golf.

Andy and his wife have three children and are the proud grandparents of four grandchildren. We are grateful for his fine contribution to this book.

The City

(left)

The Forty-Eighth State
MARK HUGHES
NIKON N90, ELITE CHROME, F-16

Statehood came to Arizona on February 14th, 1912, as it became the forty-eighth state to join the United States of America. The Arizona flag flies proudly under that of the USA, in this case on a flag pole at Canyon Lake.

(opposite)

St. Mary's Basilica
FRED YOUNG
PENTAX 645, FUJI VELVIA 50,
F-32 @ 1/30TH SECOND

Phoenix' first Catholic church originated as an adobe building in 1881. Called the "mother church of Phoenix", it was dedicated as a Basilica by Pope John Paul II in 1985. An attractive landmark in downtown Phoenix' "Copper Square" area, it stands here proudly reflecting its Spanish heritage in contrast to its more modern skyscraper neighbor.

(previous page)

City Splendor
MICHEL GASTINY
CONTAX RTS III, E100VS, F-11

An early evening view of Central Avenue taken from St. Thomas Hospital.

(above)

Gammage Auditorium
FRED YOUNG
NIKON F-801, FUJI SENSIA 100,
F-22 @ 1/30TH SECOND

Originally designed by Frank Lloyd Wright for clients in Europe, the famed architect held on to the plans when the proposed building faltered. Arizona State University was able to use them for the construction of this gem on the ASU campus in Tempe and Wright's architectural firm were the architects in charge of the project. Today "The Gammage", as it is fondly called, hosts many cultural and artistic events and is a beautiful tribute to Grady Gammage, former ASU president.

(left)

The Peacock Fountain
GEORGE ROCHELEAU
MINOLTA X-700, KODAK E100VS,
F-11 @ 4 SECONDS

The Peacock Fountain at the Phoenix Civic Center Plaza stands proudly in front of Symphony Hall. It welcomes concert and opera patrons as well as the visitor just seeking a meditative environment.

Spirit of the Dance
CARLOS L. HERNANDEZ
CANON AE-1, KODACHROME 64, F-11

John Henry Waddell, famed southwest sculptor from Sedona, created his sculpture "Dance" from 1969-1974. Conceived in four movements or acts, it celebrates the beauty of individual difference and interaction and graces the front of the Herberger Theatre in downtown Phoenix. St. Mary's Basilica is in the background.

(above)

Bank One Ballpark Under Construction

CARL S. ANDERSON

PENTAX MX, FUJI VELVIA

To all residents of The Valley of the Sun, Bank One Ballpark is fondly known as BOB. Home of the Arizona Diamondbacks, a National League franchise, it is an important part of Phoenix' vibrant downtown. Here it is shown under construction in the mid-1990's.

(opposite) Honorable Mention

Prickly Pear Cactus

KATHY HANSON

CANON A2E, FUJI VELVIA,

There are a large variety of prickly pear cactus in the Sonoran Desert, all of which bloom in the springtime when the desert comes visually alive.

(left)

Navajo Code Talkers
JOSEPH LIEST
OLYMPUS ACCURA XB70 AUTO, WALGREEN 400

Located at the northeast corner of
Thomas and Central Avenues, this
memorial is a tribute to the more than
400 Navajo Code Talkers, all United
States Marines, who bravely served
their country during World War II.
Sculpted by Doug Hyde in 1989, it
commemorates their mission which
utilized the Navajo language to create
an unbreakable secret code which the
United States and its allies used suc-
cessfully between 1942 and 1945.

(opposite)

Phoenix Old and New
PAUL SCHARBACH
MAMIYA RB-47, KODACHROME

Phoenix' old Professional Building to
the left is flanked by the modern
Valley National Bank Building which
turn reflects the Hyatt Regency Hote
Recorded close to sunset time in
downtown Phoenix.

(right)

Towering Over Central Avenue
JOSEPH LIEST
OLYMPUS ACCURA XB70 AUTO, KODAK 400

Formerly the Dial Building, now known
as the Viad Corporation Center, this
Phoenix skyscraper, normally the color
of granite, takes on a brown/red hue at
sunset. It is located in what is known
as the Central Corridor, bounded by
Seventh Avenue to the west and
Seventh Street to the east.

Taliesin West
MICHAEL ZEIHEN
CANON REBEL, KODACOLOR 200

Taliesin West is one of Frank Lloyd Wright's most famous architectural achievements. Construction began in 1937 and continued to evolve throughout his life. Wright felt that "a desert building should be nobly simple in outline, as the region itself is sculptured, should have learned from the cactus many secrets of straight line patterns for its forms." The Phoenix area contains two other well known Wright buildings, the Arizona Biltmore hotel and Gammage Auditorium on the ASU campus.

St. Mary's Basilica
PAUL SCHARBACH
RB-67, KODACHROME, F-16 @ 1/60TH

St. Mary's Basilica in early morning light, with the Valley National Bank building behind it. St. Mary's is an active Roman Catholic church where Mass is said every day. The Basilica is noted for its carillon tower and its magnificent stained glass windows, created by the Munich School of Stained Glass Art.

(opposite)

Tonto Hills Kachina
CANDACE COPELAND
ROLLIE, FUJI 100, F-5.6

This Kachina is posted as a sentry of the desert in Tonto Hills, a residential community in the northern part of The Valley. Kachina doll carvings come mostly from their Hopi heritage, though some Navajo carvers have taken up the craft as well.

Watching Over the Heard Museum
BARBARA A. MANGELS
NIKON 6006, KODAK EKTACHROME, F-6.3

Titled "Intertribal Greetings," this lime-
stone sculpture by Doug Hyde, created
in 1995, watches over Phoenix' noted
Native American Museum, The Heard.
Known for its world famous collection
of Kachina dolls, the Heard Museum on
Central Avenue captures the cultures
and arts of Native Americans and the
Southwest.

America West Arena

FRED YOUNG
PENTAX 645, FUJI VELVIA 50,
F-22 @ 1/60TH SECOND

Downtown Phoenix has managed to place many of its sports venues in close proximity to each other and to cultural centers such as the Herberger Theatre, Symphony Hall and the Orpheum Theatre. Parking is easy for all events. America West Arena is the home of the Phoenix Coyotes hockey team and the Phoenix Suns basketball franchise. It also hosts concerts of national renown.

(left)

The Orpheum Theatre

TERRY BRITTELL

CANON REBEL S, FUJICHROME 100, F-4.5

Built in 1929 and lovingly restored in recent years, the Orpheum Theatre is the last historic theatre in downtown Phoenix and in 1985 was listed in the National Register of Historic Places. The restoration process was very sensitive to retaining the building's elaborate Spanish Baroque architecture.

(opposite)

Festival of Lights

KATHY HANSON

MINOLTA X-700, FUJI VELVIA, F-22

Ahwatukee Foothills celebrates the holidays every year with its "Festival of Lights." Neighborhood volunteers string thousands of white lights on cactus and trees on Chandler Boulevard for everyone to enjoy from Thanksgiving to the New Year.

(below)

Reflections

CARLOS L. HERNANDEZ

CANON AE-1, ELITE CHROME 200, F-11

Phoenix Symphony Hall in the Phoenix Civic Plaza is the home of the Phoenix Symphony and the Arizona Opera. This cultural center features many theatrical and musical events throughout the year and its terrace provides a beautiful outdoor setting for popular festivals and events.

(above)

Monsoon Lightning Over Fountain Hills
SUSAN J. STROM
RICOH SLR, FUJI VELVIA 50, F-4

Fountain Hills lies to the east of Phoenix and Scottsdale and is often in the landing pattern of planes coming into Sky Harbor Airport. On their west to east path, monsoon storms rarely miss this rapidly growing community and surely didn't on this occasion.

(left)

Storm Over Scottsdale
SUSAN J. STROM
RICOH SLR, FUJI VELVIA 50, F-4 OR F-5.6

A September storm generates bright lightning near Shea Boulevard in Scottsdale. The intensity of these weather events often provide sharp thunder claps and strong winds.

(opposite)

Lightning Over Phoenix
SUSAN J. STROM
RICOH SLR, FUJI VELVIA 50, F-4

Looking west over Phoenix from Terminal Four at Sky Harbor Airport.

(above)

Sunrise Over Rattlesnake
MICHAEL LINDSAY
NIKON 990, DIGITAL IMAGE

Gold Canyon awakens with a sky afire over Rattlesnake Mountain. Taken at about 6:45AM, looking east.

(opposite)

Twin Sentinels
ANGELO (ANDY) VALENTI
NIKON F, KODAK GOLD 200, F-11 @ 1/250TH

Saguaro cactus can reach heights of fifty feet and weights of more than fifty tons. They provide homes for cactus wren, woodpeckers and other birds and live well beyond human life spans, counting perhaps twice as many sunrises and sunsets as we do. This is one of their best!

View From Silly Mountain
CARL S. ANDERSON
PENTAX MX, FUJI SENSIA

Apache Junction is home to a small hill called "Silly Mountain" from whose top one can see all the way to Phoenix, some forty miles to the west. At night, the Route 60 curve heading west through AJ is clearly outlined.

South Mountain Landmarks
CAROL VERNEUIL
CANON, VELVIA, F-5.6

These silhouettes of Phoenix' South Mountain transmission towers are one of the city's modern landmarks. They welcome those who arrive after sunset, bless those who leave, guide those who stay.

(opposite)

Reaching for Sky Harbor
TAMMY J. VRETTOS
NIKON N8008, FUJICHROME, F-4

Sky Harbor International Airport, home of America West airlines, is the ninth busiest airport in the United States, fifteenth busiest in the world, ranked by its passenger count. It is within a forty-five minute drive of almost any place in The Valley of the Sun.

Uptown Phoenix at Dusk
FRED YOUNG
PENTAX 645, FUJI VELVIA 50,
F-22 @ 1/15TH SECOND

Central Avenue runs on a north-south
axis, separating Phoenix and The Valley
into their east-west configurations.
Numbered roads in the East Valley are
"streets" while in the West Valley they
are "avenues." Central Avenue is a
major office and business area with a
skyline rivaling that of downtown.

A Day Ends in The Valley
JEFF SOWERS
OLYMPUS OM 2000, KODAK MAX 400

A day ends in The Valley of the Sun as seen through a railroad trestle, stressing the importance of railway traffic in the west.

The San Carlos Hotel
BRENDA M. COMBS
CANON AE1, FUJI 400, F-4

The old San Carlos Hotel, completed in 1928, was a long time gathering place for tourists as well as the stars of Hollywood. Its stately presence still contributes to all that makes Phoenix a cosmopolitan mecca in the midst of its surrounding southwest charm.

(below)

Phoenix City Hall
BRENDA M. COMBS
CANON AE1, FUJI 400, F-4

Completed in 1993 and seen here through a fisheye lens, Phoenix' new city hall is a splendid architectural addition to downtown. With a population of 1.3 million, Phoenix is America's sixth largest city. Sky Harbor Airport connects the city to the world and helps make it a state-of-the-art metropolis. The mix of Spanish and Native American cultures is clearly evident in the food, architecture and blending of languages that gives Phoenix its colorful character.

(opposite)

Heritage Square
COURTESY OF
WARREN SALINGER
PENTAX 160 IQZOOM AUTOMATIC,
KODAK GOLD 200

Heritage Square is located on Phoenix' original town site and recalls the city's Victorian past. The buildings here, that date from the late 1800's, represent the only group of residential structures from that fabled era.

In Memoriam
DICK KINNEY
NIKON 2000, FUJI 200, F-16 @ 1/500TH SECOND

The anchor of the battleship USS Arizona, sunk at Pearl Harbor on December 7th, 1941, with heavy loss of life, now rests in the Wesley Bolin Memorial Plaza across from the Arizona State Capitol.

(opposite, top)

Saguaro Lake Marina
MICHAEL ZEIHEN
CANON REBEL, KODACOLOR 100

Though Arizona has few natural lakes, there are many man-made bodies of water that are part of its systems of rivers and dams. Saguaro Lake, east of Mesa, is one of these. The marina pictured here provides a home for local boats. Rentals are available on the lake as well and are highly recommended for anyone wanting to spend some unforgettable time on the water.

(opposite, bottom)

The Desert Belle
JOHN L. WEIDMAN
CANON A-1, SEATTLE 200 ASA, F-16

The Desert Belle takes on passengers to head out on Saguaro Lake. Seen from the shore, the size of the lake is very deceiving as most of it runs out through narrower canyons where sagauro cactus and sometimes longhorn sheep watch over the boaters.

Indian Petroglyphs
JIM OEHRLEIN
OLYMPUS 0460, LIGHT AND SPEED AUTOMATIC

Many Native American tribes have left
stories of their histories behind in
hieroglyphic form. These petroglyphs
are found in the White Tank Mountains
in Maricopa County.

Papago Park Near Sunset
PAUL SCHARBACH
RB-67, FUJICHROME, F-11 @ 125TH SECOND

Mountain bikers on a trail at Phoenix'
Papago Park near sunset.

(above)

Tempe Town Lake
TINA R. JOSEPH
KONICA BIG MINI 100 APS, APS 200

Created just a few years ago, Tempe Town Lake in downtown Tempe, not far from the campus of Arizona State University, provides boating opportunities for many.

(left)

Camelback Mountain
JAMES TODD
PENTAX 4 X 6, PORTRA 160VC

No Phoenix area landmark is better known than Camelback Mountain. With views of a vibrant city in the foreground, this picture captures the dynamics of a modern urban infrastructure living in harmony with a more rural southwest.

(opposite)

Monsoon in Phoenix
JAMES TODD
PENTAX 4X6, PORTRA 160 VC

Almost always roaring in from the west as this storm is doing, Phoenix' summer monsoons bring The Valley of the Sun almost all of its annual rainfall.

Mill Avenue Bridge
DAMIAN ROBINSON
PENTAX 6 X 7, KODAK PORTIA 160, F-22

Seen here at night, the waters of Tempe Town Lake reflect the lights of the Mill Avenue Bridge. This bridge leads to the intersection of Mill and University Avenues, the center of Tempe, home of the ASU Sun Devils. Arizona State University is a major research institution, the state's largest university, with more than 50,000 students.

Midtown Phoenix
PAUL SCHARBACH
RB-67, F-11 @ 10 SECONDS

Midtown Phoenix' Central Avenue after sunset. The photograph was taken north of Osborn Street, looking south down Central Avenue. The city's lights are about to outshine the quickly fading sunlight.

(left)

Hale-Bopp Over the Sonoran Desert

GARY J. COOPER

NIKON FA, KODAK PJM-2, F-1.8

Comet Hale-Bopp graces the Sonoran Desert sky on one of its nightly passes during the spring of 1997. Taken in North Scottsdale near Desert Mountain.

(opposite)

The Great Aurora of 2001

GARY J. COOPER

NIKON F5, KODAK POARA, F-12.8

An extremely rare blazing red aurora lights up the sky in North Scottsdale during the Great Aurora of April, 2001.

Full Moon Over the Superstitions
RAYMOND S. CODERRE
CANON ELAN II, FUJI 100, F-13 @ 12 SECONDS

This photographer was at Lost Dutchman State Park in Apache Junction to shoot sunsets when a rapidly rising full moon beckoned.

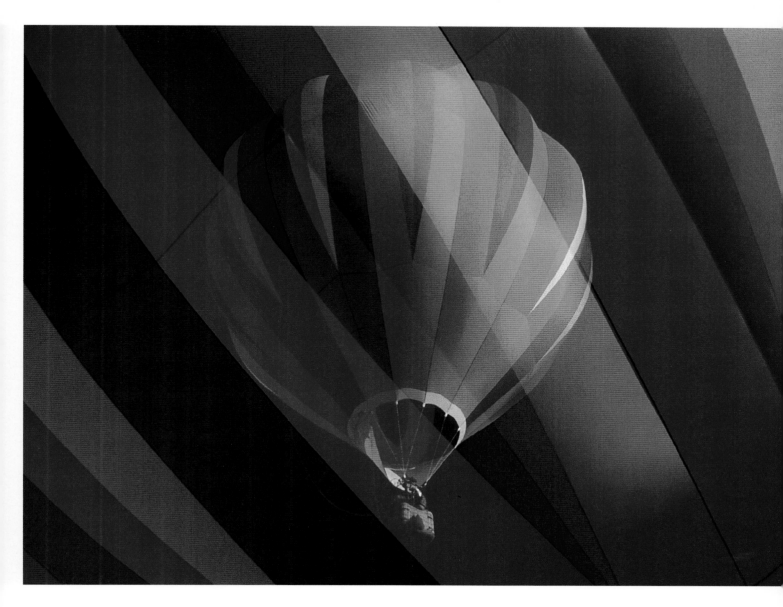

Up, Up and Away
RON L. HILDRETH
CANON ELAN, KODACHROME 64

Double exposure taken at the annual
Thunderbird Balloon Classic in
Scottsdale. The first picture taken
while the balloon was still on the
ground being filled—the second while
it was in the air.

Hot Air Balloon Festival
TAMMY J. VRETTOS
NIKON N8008, FUJICHROME, F-5.6

The Metris Thunderbird Balloon Classic held annually in Scottsdale, has been voted a top hot air ballooning event in recent years. The first hot air balloon was created by French paper makers, Joseph and Etienne Montgolfier, who were intrigued by the way smoke rises above a fire. They tested their idea with a smoke-filled balloon constructed of taffeta and rope and propelled by a straw fire which stayed aloft 41 minutes, rising to 84 feet.

(above)

A Mural Grows in Phoenix
STEWART J. KATZ
CANON REBEL X, KODAK ROYAL GOLD 200, F-16

Mural artist Steve Yazzie and local
youth, painting at the northwest corner
of Grand and Fifteenth Avenues in the
West Valley.

(opposite)

Two Bikes
LOU OATES
PENTAX 6 X 7, FUJI VELVIA

This interesting mural on the south
side of Phoenix speaks to the fact that
the climate in the valley, with sunny
days 81 percent of the time, is almost
always conducive to outdoor activities!

(top)

City of Horses
GLENDA KELLEY
NIKON N80, FUJI 100, F-5.6

There are many sculptures of horses in Scottsdale's Old Town. From this photographer's perspective, they reflect a beauty stilled but still growing.

Easy Travel
JAMES J. MCDONOUGH
CANON ECS AUTO FOCUS, KODAK 400

Known as "The West's Most Western Town," Scottsdale is home to about 220,000 people. It stretches 31 miles from south to north and covers 184.5 square miles. Over 7 million visitors come annually to its resorts, galleries, ranches, shops. And they all have to get around somehow.

Parada del Sol

ROBERT WESTERMAN

CANON ELAN II, KODAK EKTACHROME VS, F-8

Old Town Scottsdale, with its genuinely western feel, is the site of Scottsdale's annual "Parada del Sol." The rodeo, parade and other events celebrate the city's southwest heritage and its exuberant patriotism.

(above)

Outside of BOB

COURTESY OF
WARREN SALINGER
PENTAX 160 IQZOOM AUTOMATIC,
KODAK GOLD 200

One of the Phoenix skyline's newer landmarks, this is an outside view of Bank One Ballpark before a big game. It is an engineering marvel with a retractable roof, air conditioning.

(left)

Play Ball

ADAM TOLLEFSON
CANON REBEL 2000, KODAK 400

Each March the major league baseball teams from the western United States come to The Valley of the Sun for their Cactus League spring training. Here the San Francisco Giants are playing the San Diego Padres. It's a spring ritual to which valley residents look forward to all winter.

(opposite)

A View Inside BOB

JAMES TODD
PENTAX 4 X 6, PORTRA 160VC

Bank One Ballpark is home to the Arizona Diamondbacks of the National League. It features a moveable roof to assure that "play ball" will be heard no matter what tricks the weather might play. It is located in downtown Phoenix' cultural and sports center right next to America West Arena.

The Scottsdale Hyatt
JAMES TODD
PENTAX 4 X 6, PORTRA 160VC

One of a number of attractive resorts in the Greater Phoenix Area, the Scottsdale Hyatt spoils its guests with sunshine, water and golf. This is a world class resort sited on the 560 acre Gainey Ranch in North Scottsdale. Three nine-hole golf courses—the Arroyo, the Dunes and the Lakes—provide a 27 hole golfing paradise. Ten interconnecting pools assure swimmers and water people of endless aquatic fun.

The Phoenix Open
JAMES TODD
PENTAX 4 X 6, PORTRA 160VC

The annual Phoenix Open draws ever larger crowds to its fairways and greens, especially when Tiger Woods is playing. The sixteenth green is featured in this photograph.

(opposite)

Arizona Golf Scene
JAMES TODD
PENTAX 4 X 6, PORTRA 160VC

This beautiful green at the base of Pinnacle Peak symbolizes Arizona's golf scene. The sheer number of courses and the variety found inside the Grand Canyon State make it one of the best golfing destinations in the world. There are more than 275 courses from traditional to desert settings, close to 200 of them in The Valley of the Sun.

North of Mesa

LOU OATES

NOBLEX 150, FUJI VELVIA, F-16

The Salt River and Red Mountain provide a quiet background for this desert tree. With a population of more than 396,000 people, Mesa is Arizona's second largest city but this tree will never bear witness to that fact.

(above)

Agave Cactus
CAROL STUTTARD
PENTAX, KODAK 200 ASA

Each Agave Cactus plant blooms only once, then dies. This one is in Phoenix' Desert Botanical Garden. Founded in 1937, this unique garden displays one of the most extensive collections of desert plants in the world.

(left)

Wild Prickly Pear Cactus Flowers
MICHAEL A. GEROW, JR.
NIKON F5, FUJI SENSIA II 100, F-16

Early morning light brings these beavertail cactus flowers to their fullest beauty. A member of the prickly pear family of cacti, beavertail are so called because their pads resemble a beaver's tail.

(opposite)

Chain Fruit Cholla
CAROL STUTTARD
PENTAX, KODAK 200 ASA

Frequently called "Jumping Cholla" for the way it drops its short terminal joints on the ground in order to reproduce (they are extremely sharp), this cholla cactus dwells in the flat desert, often forming large forests of many plants.

The Mountains

(above)

The Rugged Superstitions
GEORGE ROCHELEAU
MINOLTA X-700, KODAK E100VS

Popular for hiking and camping, the Superstition Wilderness Area, of which Superstition Mountain is a part, contains some 242 square miles or 159,780 acres of Arizona's rugged desert mountain terrain. Some mountain peaks tower 6,000 plus feet above sea level and deep canyons disect this vast wilderness region.

(previous page)

Four Peaks in Winter White
CARL S. ANDERSON
PENTAX MX, FUJI SENSIA

At an altitude of 7,645 feet, Four Peaks Mountain is often clothed in winter white while the desert valley below is bathed in milder temperatures of sixty to seventy degrees that are more "Phoenix-like." The mountain, east of Phoenix on the way to Payson, is an ever present landmark.

At the Top of the Peralta Trail
EDDIE ELLIS
MINOLTA 7X1, KODAK EKTACHROME 100, F-19

The Peralta Trail has become one of the
most used hiking trails in the Superstition Wilderness. It was named after
the Peraltas, a Mexican family who
sold the directions to a rich Superstition Mountain gold mine to Jacob
Waltz after the end of the Mexican-
American War.

**Poppies and Lupines on
Squaw Peak**
MARK HUGHES
NIKON N90, FUJI VELVIA, F-5.6

With the slightest hint of blue amongst
the yellow, lupines and Mexican poppies interface on the Squaw Peak trail.
Part of the Phoenix Mountain Preserve,
Squaw Peak Park features a 1.2 mile
trail to the peak's summit.

(above)

Springtime at Lost Dutchman
KATHY HANSON
CANON A2E, FUJI PROVIA 100F

Jacob Waltz, the "Lost Dutchman" for
whom the park is named, entered the
Superstition Mountains in search of
gold, prospecting there from 1868 to
1886. Many legends have evolved from
his time there but his mine has never
been found.

The Salt River
KATHY HANSON
CANON A2E, FUJI VELVIA, F-22

The Salt River flows through the East
Valley, providing many recreational
opportunities, including boating,
fishing and tubing. This view of the
Salt River includes Four Peaks in
the distance.

(above)

Weaver's Needle
EDDIE ELLIS
MINOLTA 7 X 1, KODAK EKTACHROME 100, F-22

Named after Powell Weaver, mountain
man, guide, prospector and early
Arizona pioneer, the Weaver's Needle
has often been associated with the
mining tales of Jacob Waltz, the "Lost
Dutchman." It appeared on military
maps as early as 1853, almost two
decades before Superstition Mountain
was noted.

(following page)

The Ever Changing Mountain
MICHAEL A. GEROW, JR.
NIKON F5, FUJI VELVIA, F-19

When the sun sets in the west and its
receding light illuminates Superstition
Mountain, the monolith takes on an
ethereal quality, changing color constantly. Shadows paint whole moun-
tainsides in preparation for the night
to come.

Hedgehog Splendor
ELLIOTT MEYERSON
NIKON 8008, AGFACHROME, F-8

Though the cactus in Arizona always bloom as spring hits the desert floor, each time it happens it's a treat all over again. Here a hedgehog cactus is in its full glory.

Four Peaks at the End of the Day
MICHAEL A. GEROW, JR.
NIKON F5, FUJI SENSIA II 100, F-11

Golden hour nearing its end at Four Peaks Mountain, east of Phoenix.

(opposite)

Beauty of the Night
EDDIE ELLIS
MINOLTA 7X1, KODAK EKTACHROME 100, F-5.6

Not forgetting to look behind you is a good rule for all photographers. This moon rising over craggy Superstition peaks is the reward for remembering.

(opposite, top)

Full Moon Rise, Lost Dutchman State Park

BETH MCCULLOUGH-RUSSELL
CANON EOS A2E, FUJI SENSIA II 100, F-3.5

Teddy bear cholla cactus in the foreground and the Superstitions further back provide this stage for a full moon rising. Lost Dutchman State Park is named for the "Lost Dutchman" gold mine, the location of which Jacob Waltz, the Dutchman, took with him to his grave in 1891.

(opposite, bottom)

Early Evening in the Superstitions

MARK HUGHES
NIKON N90, FUJI VELVIA, F-22

If at the end of a full day hiking, Jacob Waltz' Lost Dutchman mine has still eluded you, take solace in the beauty of an early Superstition evening.

(above)

Superstition Beauty

BETH MCCULLOUGH-RUSSELL
MAMIYA RANGEFINDER, FUJI VELVIA, F-8 @ 1/125TH

Chuparosa and brittlebush act as a floral runner for the majesty of Superstition Mountain as it reaches for the heavens. The early farmers of the Salt River Valley who grew hay for the army at Ft. McDowell in the late 1860's constantly heard stories from the Pima Indians about how they feared this mountain. The farmers thought the Pimas were superstitious about the mountain, hence its name.

(previous page)

Night Comes to the Superstitions
EDDIE ELLIS
MINOLTA 7 X 1, KODAK EKTACHROME 100, F-19

Superstition Mountain in the distant
past was a thousand feet higher than it
is today. Uplift, subsidence, resurgence
and erosion have all played a role in
shaping this heroic mountain.

(above)

Perseverence
BRENDA M. COMBS
MINOLTA 7000, FUJI SENSIA 200, F-8

A lone sunflower family member grows
amidst the rock in Dreamy Draw Park.

(opposite)

Make a Wish
EDDIE ELLIS
MINOLTA 7 X 1, KODAK EKTACHROME 100, F-4

A deceased saguaro in wishbone for-
mation has undoubtedly enticed many
hikers to make a wish here. The western face of the Superstitions is in the
background.

**Wildflowers and
Superstition Mountain**

TAMMY J. VRETTOS

NIKON N8008, KODAK GOLD 100, F-8

Though these wildflowers may not
divulge their presence, mule deer,
javelinas, mountain lions, bobcats,
coyotes, plus a variety of birds, reptiles
and amphibeans coexist in this fragile
desert eco-system.

(above)

No Compete Clause
MARY BELL
CANON A-1, KODAK 200, AUTOMATIC

Touching down atop the Vulture Peak Mountains, this rainbow coexists in peaceful splendor with a saguaro cactus, creating a picture as unique and powerful as the Sonoran Desert can offer.

(right)

Pot of Gold
MARK HUGHES
NIKON N90, FUJI VELVIA, F-6

After a rain on Squaw Peak Mountain you feel that you're on the way to finding that proverbial pot of gold at the end of the rainbow!

(above)

Spring Wildflowers
GEORGE ROCHELEAU
MINOLTA X-570, KODAK E100VS

The mountains and the dead tree in
the background, stressing Arizona's
rugged nature, are softened immedi-
ately by this display of spring wildflowers. Taken by the Salt River, near
Saguaro Lake.

(opposite, top)

Hedgehogs in Bloom
TAMMY J. VRETTOS
NIKON N8008, KODAK GOLD 100, F-4

Hedgehog cactus in bloom at the base
of Superstition Mountain in Apache
Junction.

(opposite, bottom)

**Vibrant Superstition
Mountain Valley**
TAMARA JOHNSTONE
SONY DIGITAL DSC-570

Superstition Mountain in profile with
its famed Flat Iron in perfect view,
backed by the Goldfield Mountains in
the distance. Spring wildflowers and
a golf course fairway all contribute to
create an outstanding Arizona
panorama.

(above)

Canyon Lake
TALLIS KUMPIS
NIKON N-80, KODAK GOLD 100, F-11

Serene beauty blankets Canyon Lake,
tucked into the Superstitions and a
part of the Salt River Project that
brings water to Phoenix and The Valley.
It's a great place to fish and boat.

(left)

Overlooking Boyce Thompson Arboretum
LEROY J. SMITH

This desert lake overlooks the Boyce Thompson
Arboretum, Arizona's oldest and largest botanical garden. Located at the eastern end of The
Valley of the Sun, the arboretum houses miles
of nature paths that wind their way through
towering trees, an otherwordly cactus collection, charming herb and rose gardens and
alongside a babbling brook.

(opposite)

Arizona Windmill
LOU OATES
PENTAX 6 X 7, FUJI PROVIA, F-16

Though it's hard to tell when cattle last drank
the water this windmill pumped, its structure
still speaks to the ranching so important to the
west. It is located at the eastern extremity of
The Valley of the Sun, near Picketpost
Mountain on Route 60 east.

A Desert Blanket
GEORGE ROCHELEAU
MINOLTA X-570, KODAK E100VS, F-11

Mexican gold poppies blanket the desert, covering the scars of a previous fire, showing the magic of nature healing itself. Taken in the Tonto National Forest near Saguaro Lake.

(opposite, top)

Power of the Mountain
COURTESY OF
WARREN SALINGER
PENTAX 160 IQZOOM AUTOMATIC,
KODAK GOLD 200

This panoramic view of the western face of Superstition Mountain accents the sheer power this Phoenix area symbol exerts over the East Valley.

(opposite, bottom)

A Golden Carpet
COURTESY OF
WARREN SALINGER
PENTAX 160 IQZOOM AUTOMATIC,
KODAK GOLD 200

Mexican poppies and brittlebush roll out in golden splendor in a spring desert spectacle that flows northeastward towards Four Peaks mountain in the distance.

(opposite)

Last Light in the Mountains
BETH MCCULLOUGH-RUSSELL
CANON EOS A2E, FUJI SENSI II, F-3.5 @ 1/60TH

Lost Dutchman State Park provides the setting for a last light photograph featuring the yellow flowers of the prolific brittlebush as well as the red blooms of the chuparosa. Stems of the latter, member of the honeysuckle family, are soft and covered with velvety hairs. The plant attracts many species of hummingbirds.

(above)

The First Sunset
MICHAEL LINDSAY
PENTAX 110

Coming down the Petroglyph Trail in Gold Canyon at the foothills of the Superstitions, looking to the southeast. The cone shaped mountain is near the Casa Grande ruins in Coolidge. This was the photographer's first Arizona sunset, one for the memory books.

(above)

Ocotillo Cactus Near Full Bloom
TAMARA JOHNSTONE
SONY DIGITAL DSC-570

The long stems of the ocotillo cactus, often reaching heights of six feet or more, are a familiar sight in the Sonoran Desert. Ocotillos usually flower between March and May, in time for the northward migration of hummingbirds. The waxy, red, tubular flowers attract many other insects and birds as well.

(opposite)

Spring Splendor
MICHAEL LINDSAY
NIKON 990, DIGITAL IMAGE

Mexican poppies on the east side of Dinosaur Mountain. Taken in March at about 9:35AM in a spring bountiful in desert wildflowers due to winter months that brought higher than average rainfall.

Syphon Draw Ravine
MICHAEL LINDSAY
NIKON 990, DIGITAL IMAGE

One of the many hiking trails in Lost Dutchman State Park, the Syphon Draw Trail is the easiest way to the top of Superstition Mountain, but not on the morning after a major snowfall like this!

(opposite, top)

Returning From the Flat Iron
MICHAEL LINDSAY
NIKON 990, DIGITAL IMAGE

Spring snows in the Superstition Mountains are not all that rare but the depth of this snowfall made it unusual. The Flat Iron is near the summit of Superstition Mountain, at an altitude of more than 5,000 feet. The city of Apache Junction is in the valley below.

(opposite, bottom)

Winter in North Scottsdale
IRIS PESCHEL
OLYMPUS AUTOMATIC

Sometimes there is winter in North Scottsdale. This is Pinnacle Peak Mountain, taken from Happy Valley Road east of Pima Road. Snow scenes in this area rarely last more than a day. This was an April storm and was gone in a flash.

The West

(above)

Bareback on Slice
BETH MCCULLOUGH-RUSSELL
CANON EOS A2E, FUJI SENSIA II,
F-8 @ 1/125TH *(above)*
F-5.6 @ 1/125TH *(opposite)*

Many trails in Lost Dutchman State
Park are shared by horses and humans.
Often, the riders ride bareback as
Rhonda Sherry does in this instance
on her horse, Slice. All of this old
west activity occurs within minutes of
modern city life, making Phoenix and
The Valley of the Sun such an unsual
habitat.

(previous page)

Western Superstition Face
EDDIE ELLIS
MINOLTA 7X1, KODAK EKTACHROME 100, F-22

Formed by volcanic upheaval some 29
million years ago, during the tertiary
period of geological time, Superstition
Mountain has been slowly eroded over
millions of years by running water
and wind to form the mountain we
see today.

Native American Hoop Dancers
KATHY SCHMIDT

Every year the Heard Museum spon-
sors its annual Native American Hoop
Dancing Contest to the acclaim of
those fortunate enough to watch.
Twenty-one federally recognized
Native American tribes exist in Arizona
with a population of about 300,000.
Among the most highly visible are the
Navajo, many of whom live on their
large reservation in northeastern
Arizona that includes Monument Valley
and Canyon de Chelly. If you let it,
Native American culture and wisdom
can touch your life every day you are in
the Grand Canyon State. It's a huge
fringe benefit, so let it!

(above)

Saguaro at Sunset
TAMMY J. VRETTOS
NIKON N8008, FUJICHROME, F-2.8

Saguaro cactus at sunset, taken at the Desert Botanical Garden in Papago Park, Phoenix, located on 1,200 acres of rolling desert hills and rugged mountains.

(opposite)

Desert Globe Mallow
TAMMY J. VRETTOS
NIKON N8008, KODAK GOLD 100, F-4

Several species of globe mallow are common in the desert. Most have scalloped leaves and peachy pink flowers as these do, photographed in Deer Valley.

(above)

Rodeo
TAMMY J. VRETTOS
NIKON N8008, FUJICHROME, F-4

Drive north on Scottsdale Road towards Carefree and Cave Creek and you will find Rawhide, an authentically recreated western town. And, if you're lucky, you'll be there at rodeo time when cowgirls and cowboys still show off their wrangling skills as this steer wrestling scene proves.

(previous page)

Superstition Sunrise
ROBERT J. KONIECZNY, SR.
NIKON 8008, KODAK GOLD 100, F-5.6

Taken just south of Tortilla Flats on the Apache Trail, deep in the Superstitions, this is one of the beautiful sunrises that excites the people of The Valley of the Sun.

(above)

Heaven's Artwork
MALLORY VICTOR
ADVANTAX AUTOMATIC, 200 ASA

In front of the photographer's home at the end of an August day. No human hands could duplicate this sunset scene.

(right)

Welcome to Apache Junction
CARL S. ANDERSON
PENTAX P21P, FUJI VELVIA

With a population of 32,000 people, Apache Junction, known by its famous prospector logo, straddles Route 60 in the East Valley. Once remarkable for the many RV parks located within its boundaries, the city, called the gateway to the Superstitions, is building more permanent residential housing at a rapid pace.

Desert Bird of Prey

TAMMY J. VRETTOS

NIKON N8008, KODAK GOLD 100, F-4

Desert skies are home to many birds of prey such as hawks, eagles, falcons. Here a Prairie Falcon recovers at the Adobe Mountain Wildlife Refuge in Deer Valley.

(opposite)

When You Reach the Fork in the Cactus, Take It!

CYNTHIA CRONIG

MINOLTA 3XI, FUJICHROME, F-16

Comfortably perched in the fork of a deceased saguaro cactus, this desert bird has found a great place to rest. Saguaros live for more than 100 years and don't grow branches till they are well over 40. The ribs seen here indicate the fluted construction of this giant cactus, enabling it to expand as its roots soak up water when available, and to contract as the moisture is used.

(above)

Cave Creek Saguaro
CANDACE COPELAND
ROLLIE 35S, KODAK 200

The many arms on this saguaro cactus indicate its long life. Shown here reaching for the sky in Cave Creek, the branching on this cactus has occurred as it does in most saguaros, rising from one level on the plant, high above the ground.

(opposite)

Monsoon Clouds Rolling In
CARL S. ANDERSON
PENTAX MX, FUJI VELVIA

The monsoon clouds of summer roll in over the desert east of Apache Junction with saguaro cactus eager for the coming rain.

Right Place, Right Time

IAN GRANT-WHYTE

MINOLTA MAXXUM, FUJICOLOR, F-1.4

While poolside at Marriott's Camelback Inn on a late fall afternoon, the Arizona sky exploded for this lucky photographer, the colors seeming to reach unreachable peaks. Right place, right time.

Stormy Moon Rising
MIKE MCCLURE
MAMIYA 645, FUJI VELVIA, F-8

Sunsets, thunderstorms and rising full moons are all dramatic sights in Phoenix. Occasionally, as in this picture taken at Arrowhead Ranch in Glendale, they all happen at the same time.

Lupines by the Highway
ELLIOTT MEYERSON
NIKON N80, FUJI ASTIA, F-22

Seeds of desert lupine germinate on as
little as half an inch of rain, providing
wildflower accents to Arizona highways
even if rainfall is poor. This display, just
outside of Apache Junction, is quite
obviously plentiful, rich and a great
addition to this desert roadside.

Desert at Sunrise
TAMARA JOHNSTONE
SONY DIGITAL DSC-570, F-2

The desert in bloom! Gold Canyon,
Arizona at sunrise.

Cattle Graze in the East Valley
KIMBERLYN KEATON
PENTAX K100, KODAK 400

Cattle grazing off South Ellsworth Road
in Queen Creek prove that ranching is
still an important part of life in Arizona
and The Valley of the Sun. However,
Arizona's rapidly growing population
does threaten this bucolic scene.

Arizona Agriculture
JAMES TODD
PENTAX 4X6, PORTRA 160VC

Arizona is well known for its three
"C's" which stand for cattle, cotton and
copper, all important parts of the
state's economy. Fields fertile thanks
to irrigation are never far from the ever
present mountains.

Apacheland Movie Ranch
COURTESY OF
WARREN SALINGER
PENTAX 160 IQZOOM AUTOMATIC,
KODAK GOLD 200

Named after the rich history of the Apache Indians who once roamed this area, Apacheland Movie Ranch is situated on 85 acres of pristine Sonoran Desert land in Gold Canyon. "Death Valley Days", hosted by former President Ronald Reagan, was one of many western TV series and full length movies filmed here. Elvis Presley filmed "Charro" here. Rex Allen, Roy Rogers, Dale Evans were just some of the other stars who worked here.

(left)

The Sheriff of Goldfield
JANET KELLY
NIKON N-70, ASA 200, F-11

The Goldfield of today is the home of Ghost Town, one of Arizona's famous western attractions, This sheriff is one of the lawmen of the community. Three to five thousand people once lived here, all lured by the prospect that "there was gold in them hills!"

(opposite)

Ghost Town's Mammoth Saloon
KATHY SCHMIDT

When Goldfield was a booming mining community there were three saloons, a hotel, boarding houses and a general store. There were fifty working mines in the district! You can still ride up to the Mammoth Saloon today, tie up your horse and order a steak. And you can still pan for gold at the reconstructed section of the Old Mammoth Mine.

Wrangler at Work
MARY BELL
CANON A-1, KODAK 200, F-8

This ranch land skirts the northwest side of the White Tank Mountain Range in Maricopa County. After an all-day ride, this wrangler will sleep on the ground, cook over a camp fire, forget to shave, curse the rain. Tomorrow he will tend to the cattle again and each day that he lives his ranch life will enrich the west's cowboy lore of which he is so important a part.

Don't Call Me Pig!
MARY BELL
CANON A-1, KODAK 200, AUTOMATIC

This Javelina mother protecting her baby is an oft-repeated scene in the Sonoran Desert. Feeding on desert plants, especially prickly pear cactus, javelinas are not dangerous unless they feel threatened. Though they look, walk and often smell like pigs, their ancestry is rodent and they do not like to be called pigs!

(opposite)

Desert Destiny
CANDACE COPELAND
ROLLIE 35S, FUJI, F-8

Cattle skulls hung from this dead saguaro cactus, somewhere in Cave Creek, north of Scottsdale, underscore two things: that ranching is still an important part of Arizona life and that the desert is often hard and unforgiving.

(above)

Bubba Wins!
ELLIOTT MEYERSON
NIKON 8008, FUJI PROVIA, F-8

Bubba wins a Fender guitar and could not be happier! The Fender was raffled at the Phoenix Blues Society's "Blues Blast" at the Mesa Amphitheatre.

(opposite)

Red Hot Chilli Peppers
CANDACE COPELAND
ROLLIE 35S, FUJI, F-5.6

Red chilli peppers add spice to any desert landscape and to many south-western foods. These were spotted in Cave Creek, right next door to Carefree, which, as its name indicates, is one laid back Arizona community.

(above)

Blowing the Rain Away
MICHAEL LINDSAY
NIKON 990, DIGITAL IMAGE

Facing Dinosaur Mountain after a summer storm, sky clearing, winds blowing the rain away.

(opposite)

A Rising Sun
DICK KINNEY
NIKON 2000, FUJI SUPERA 200, F-5.6

A rising sun silhouettes these beautiful saguaros at daybreak. This photograph was taken at the White Tank Mountains west of Phoenix at 5AM.

Carl S. Anderson
62 East Juniper Street
Mesa, AZ 85201
Azphotocreations@cs.com
3, 18, 32, 66–67, 109, 113

Mary Bell
POB 57
Morristown, AZ 85342
RanchAz@aol.com
85, 122(2)

Terry Brittell
550 East McKellips Road
Mesa, AZ 85203
26

Raymond S. Coderre
702 South Meridian # 629
Apache Junction, AZ 85220
50

Brenda M. Combs
9502 North 15th Avenue
220
Phoenix, AZ 85021
burnie8@uswest.net
37(2), 82

Gary J. Cooper
9920 East Quarry Trail
Scottsdale, AZ 85262
aao000@aol.com
back cover, 46, 47

Candace Copeland
POB 3486
Carefree, AZ 85377
Copelandart@earthlink.net
22, 112, 123, 125

Cynthia Cronig
47 Lakeside Drive, East
Centerville, MA 02632
Croworld@mediaone.net
110

Eddie Ellis
285 West Bruce Avenue
Gilbert, AZ 85233
*back cover, 5, 69,73, 77,
80–81, 83, 98–99*

Michel Gastiny
357 East Thomas Road
#A-106
Phoenix, AZ 85012-3210
3, 12-13

Michael A. Gerow, Jr.
1378 East Butler Circle
Chandler, AZ 85225
64, 74–75, 76

Ian Grant-Whyte
5635 East Lincoln Road #150
Paradise Valley, AZ 85253
grantwhyte@Bigfoot.com
114

Kathy Hanson
15227 South 14th Avenue
Phoenix, AZ 85045
Khanson@sfamipec.com
19, 27, 71, 72

Carlos L. Hernandez
10505 West Signal
Butte Circle
Sun City, AZ 85373
17, 26

Ron L. Hildreth
5309 West Brown
Glendale, AZ 85302
rhildret@peoriaud.K12.AZ.US
51

Mark Hughes
2210 East Cactus Wren Drive
Phoenix, AZ 85020
All-Light@msn.com
14, 70, 78, 85

Tamara Johnstone
39 Cobblestone Lane
San Carlos, CA 94070
ryant@surgery.ucsf.edu
87, 94, 117

Tina R. Joseph
2141 East University # 34
Tempe, AZ 85281
barbie420x@netzero.alt
42

Stewart J. Katz
631 South Peppertree Drive
Gilbert, AZ 85296
54

Kimberlyn Keaton
1322 South Dodge Court
Gilbert, AZ 85233
KLHK26@aol.com
118

Glenda Kelley
4973 North Reggae Road
Maricopa, AZ 85239
56

Janet Kelly
2311 Leisure World
Mesa, AZ 85206
Hhejan@aol.com
120

Dick Kinney
6227 North Litchfield Road
Litchfield, AZ 85340
38, 127

Robert J. Konieczny, Sr.
3630 East Cody Circle
Gilbert, AZ 85234
robkphoto@earthlink.net
106–107

Tallis Kumpis
2433 West Main Street
Mesa, AZ 85201
tkumpis@hotmail.com
88

Harmon Leslie
315 East Jacaranda Street
Mesa, AZ 85201
hleslie@msn.com
48

Joseph Liest
60 West Lynwood Street # 2
Phoenix, AZ 85003
20(2)

Michael Lindsay
5065 South Louie LaMour
Drive
Gold Canyon, AZ 85219
GoldCanyonPhoto@aol.com
1, 30, 93, 95, 96, 97, 126

Mike McClure
6327 West Bluefield Avenue
Glendale, AZ 85308
mcclurem@earthlink.net
115

Beth McCullough-Russell
5135 North Placita Solitaria
Tucson, AZ 85750
Russell@RTO.com
78, 79, 92, 100, 101

James J. McDonough
2830 Burnt Oak Drive
San Antonio, TX 78232
JMcDonough@SATX.RR.com
56

Barbara A. Mangels
2015 West Summit Place
Chandler, AZ 85224-1169
phoart3@juno.com
back cover, 24

Elliott Meyerson
834 East Estevan
Apache Junction, AZ 85219
Atoast@Gateway.net
76, 116, 124

Lou Oates
2170 East Alameda Drive
Tempe, AZ 85282
louoates@mich.com
54–55, 62–63, 89

Jim Oehrlein
7300 North 51st Avenue
F-99
Glendale, AZ 85301
40

Iris Peschel
8056 East Lariat
Scottsdale, AZ 85255
ipeschel@hotmail.com
97

Damian Robinson
2506 North 7th Street
Phoenix, AZ 85006
44

George Rocheleau
2425 East Inverness
Mesa, AZ 85204
georvki@uswest.net
16, 68–69, 86–87, 91

Warren Salinger
8743 East Saguaro Blossom
Gold Canyon, AZ 85219
wasal@igc.org
36, 58, 90(2), 120

Paul Scharbach
926 East Keim
Phoenix, AZ 85014
*front cover, 7, 8–9, 21, 23,
41, 45*

Kathy Schmidt
813 North Granite Street
Gilbert, AZ 85224
3, 102(2), 103, 121

LeRoy J. Smith
305 South Val Vista # 297
Mesa, AZ 85204
roysmithxx@aol.com
88

Jeff Sowers
8564 West Palo Verde
Peoria, Arizona 85345
35

Susan J. Strom
12270 North Chama # 1
Fountain Hills, AZ 85268
Stormavenue@hotmail.com
28(2), 29

Carol Stuttard
10225 North 130th Way
Scottsdale, AZ 85259
64, 65

James Todd
2506 North 7th Street
Phoenix, AZ 85006
Aeria@Goodnet.com
42, 43, 59, 60(2), 61, 119

Adam Tollefson
3620 East Fudigo Circle
Mesa, AZ 85205
AZAT85@aol.com
58

Angelo (Andy) Valenti
8704 East Jumping Cholla
Drive
Gold Canyon, AZ 85219
Andyv3@juno.com
11, 31

Carol Verneuil
33 Woody Lane
Westport, CT 06880
jverneui@optonline.net
32

Mallory Victor
1923 East Jensen Street
Mesa, AZ 85203
Malbo03@aol.com
3, 109

Tammy J. Vrettos
547 South Cholla Street
Gilbert, AZ 85233
*33, 52, 53, 84, 87, 104,
105, 108, 111*

John L. Weidman
1025 North Arroya
Mesa, AZ 85205
johnweidman@aol.com
39

Robert Westerman
7521 North 46th Avenue
Glendale, AZ 85301
rwphoto@quest.net
49, 56–57

Fred Young
1250 West Grove Parkway
2143
Tempe, AZ 85283
phlens33@cs.com
15, 16, 25, 34

Michael Zeihen
9345 North 92nd Street
116
Scottsdale, AZ 85258
23, 39